# STRANGERS
## TO
# *soulmates*

*a poetic journey for lovers*

*by*
*Lola & Tigre Pickett*

*selections*
*2012—2018*

MAY THESE WORDS
IGNITE LOVE IN
YOUR LIFE.

*tyler + lola*

## written for

all the lovers
across great divides
of space and time

all the seekers
of true love,
your
one-in-seven-billion
is
out
there.

# table of contents

**the beginning.**

one hundred hours
after we met
you sent
the first poem

twenty six days later
you left for the rainforest

my life
torn apart for you like cotton candy
so sweet
i never felt the ripping

9 months of distance
pages of verses

the invisible future
unraveled infinitely
a feathered void

one day
we leapt into the abyss

*enter into the story of us*
*we didn't know*
*we were writing*

it started
with
this...

**meanings of lives.**

let's take a walk,
and discuss
meanings of lives.

how the other
have-nots live, or
how lucky we are.

our energies,
perspectives
mingle and mesh.

vaguely similar
setups, drastically
different outcomes.

a chance to
grow with and
love another.

crossing into
territories unknown,
exhilarating.

anticipating your
beauty manifested
in my reality.

knowing that
the best
is yet to come.

**waiting.**

energy trembles,
anticisyncopation.

flying on your threads,
fantastical : ecstatical.

your thoughts kept me
in bliss this lazy morning.

waiting for your embrace
soft kisses of grace.

## history.

language fails me once again
and so I take page to pen
and scribble scattered thoughts of when

it was I asked for this
for such a strong virtual sense
of impending interconnected bliss

and of course I got an answer
in a dreamy thoughtful dancer

who even though I do not know
I have a sense we've been here though

among the trees and leaves perhaps
or mingling as cells or slats
of wood across a creaking bow
thank goodness we are human now

**you.**

are poetry

your energy flows
over me
like rivulets
over stones

i wait
anticipate
my breath abates

i grow warm
with longing

awakening
a fire within

your skin
your taste
your face
an embrace

that leaves me
shaky
and
salty
and
hungry

for more

i feel the rhythm of
you
it lingers
and my fingers
trace
your shapes

memorizing
every inch

tantalizing my
petals
to open to the rain

**free flowing.**

a breeze sweeps in, gentle. beautiful.
lifting my shirt it tickles and caresses.
where does it come from? should i care?
from nature born, to dust we return.

questions arise, answers clarify,
emotions heighten, love flows.
now, i sit with this breeze, nourishing,
exciting, all-encompassing.

in truth, i invited this gust of life in,
i knocked on its door.  i beckoned.
i knew its history, its direction,
so why am i reversing roles?

the love, the connections,
the laughter and joy i feel are all true.
but, i still tremble when deeper thought
fills my mind of how karma plays her game.

i believe this breeze, i feel it in my bones.
it lifts my spirit and fills my heart.
all i hope is that my embrace of its caress
brings only happiness, not pain.

**how i want.**

you.
your lips, your eyes.
your touch, your caress.

my mind mingles thoughts
of your embrace as i trace
our body lines entwining.

only hours more till
my fantasy meets
our reality.

**drowsy.**

i lay in a pool of myself.
drifting in and out of drowsy sleep.
feeling your phantasy
move over my skin
in the softest waves.

**before we meet again.**

in that tenuous space
between potential
and manifest
i wait for him.

dreaming of silken skin
between my teeth
gently
devouring
every
last
inch.

the universe explodes
inside me
and i am born again
or maybe
for the first time.

who do i thank
for his appearance?

be it stars or fate
or simply the web
that caught us both;

wings glistening in the sun
as we writhe against the strands

and cling to each other
to thrive
another day.

**rainticipation.**

i wait
for you
my heart
beat
syncopating
with
rainy
percussion

rivulets
r
 u
  n
down
the
window

drumming my
mind
into
heady readiness

my body
lies heavy
in the bed
s
i
n
k
i
n
g

down
down

as my
fingers
r-u-n
and
tremble

against
the
wetness
you
always
leave
me
with

**rhythm.**

you are a
sanguine song
pumping thumping
through my veins
loosing my reins
and leaving me
unbridled.

under your body
mine writhes
and comes alive
and comes
and
comes
and
comes.

perhaps two plus
two always
equalled five
and i never understood
why.

**celestial guides.**

twinkling, fiery, atomic furnaces
what do you know?

did you see these terrestrial bodies
colliding before their birth?

did you orchestrate their encounter
like so many fates before?

or is it only your colossal size
that guides their romance?

whichever manner you have,
or haven't, participated in is mute.

i only ask out of curiosity,
in search of a paint or wash.

something to give value
to this amorphous affair.

anything to distinguish their
dazzling and palpable love.

Dear Tiger,

I miss you. I miss hearing your breathing deepen before you fall asleep (usually seconds after we've stopped talkingkissingloving- touching).

I look at the sky, clouded over. The stars behind it – the same ones you see – are hidden, yet I know they shine on you as I write this.

I haven't cried.

It makes your absence too real. Instead I pretend it's just another day or so until I'll wake up next to you again.

Everything reminds me of you. Every joke, every lovers' glance, every song, every single thing I lay my eyes on turns into a taunt of you. Teasing the tears that prick my lids, refusing to spill over.

I am not sad. The tears I am running from are those of sheer amazement and joy at the fact of your existence. To have you in my lifemindheart fuels my soul, feeds my imagination, and makes my body yearn for yours.

I sleep with your face just beyond reach, with your voice in my head, and visions of you driving us through the desert; winding through the washed sunlit expanses as my heart explodes and you read my mind with a grin and a slight shake of your head.

It's been one day (37.5 hours to be exact) since I kissed you good- bye and careened by your car on the freeway so I didn't have to watch you leave.

What will the next unknown bring?

Missing you is the best pain I've felt in a long time.

Love,
Le Fox

Dear Tiger,

I was re-reading our email chain... It doesn't contain the entire picture of course – we're missing texts, facebook messages, etc...

Our first exchange was on 2/27/12.

My head spins as I read the tone in our messages shift from friendly curiosity to witty banter, to flirting, to outright fiery desire and declarations of love.

The messages are in one of three languages... French, Spanish, or English. We have inside jokes, nicknames, photos, hundreds of conversations. Three weeks of sporadic hours spent lustily consuming every detail, every inch of skin, and devouring each other before time ran out.

Two phone calls.

At first glance, it seems lightning fast.

Yet YOUthis spurn me to take actions I've been avoiding for years.

I watch as my mind tries first to comprehend what's happened... To rationalize and form words to explain myself to myself. Then, I watch the doubts filter through.

My mind attempts to methodically destroy it [whatever it is] before it ever has a chance to hurt me or get off the ground.

I watch, but I don't listen to the idle thoughtchatter.
For, what does my mind know of love or fate?

I'm dying to go to sleep... because, perhaps our souls somehow find each other and play while our bodies rest. Perhaps they've been playing like that for decades.

Dulces Sueños,
Le Fox

**high.**

i dowse myself
in sensations of you.

music drumsthrums
throbbing though
my mind and veins

until again
i come
alive
come
again.

every sight
smell
sound...

...the list of you
reads like
the minutia
of any life

to me
these tiny details
feel significant
succulent
like soul food.

i gather my
memories
and weave them
into the basket
that lifts me
to the novastars

carried away
by your
helium hypnosis.

## homecoming.

sometimes
coming back home
is a gritty reminder
that
your true home
is not out there;

rather
it lives
inside
the moonly
madness
of your
wild
beating
heart.

there
is where
you've nestled
into the
craggy
crevices
of my
former
disillusionment
and
current
state
of wonder.

there
is where
i find you
each
night as

my heart
slows
and i
drift into
sleepy
sheets

silky
against
my skin.

**mists of memory.**

my mind meanders,
a peek there,
a recollection here.

i'm searching for you
in the mist of memories.

faces, moments, pleasures,
mix and jumble as if
in a blender.

i've found you for but
a brief moment.

the present takes
me back to now,
my heart wants then.

**as the night wanes.**

i trace the nape
of your neck
in my memory lanes

savory conversation
licks at my skin
like campfire flames

words are spicy
like sangiovese
on our tongues

red-gold-threads
of provocative passion
beckon me

merging me into a life
ecstatic, so ripe
as i taste the fruit

the evening fades
and you are sleeping
i smile into the dark
unknown

**enwrapme.**

take your thread,
weave me into
these intricate
patterns of
hemorrhaging lust.

stitch me through,
sink it deep,
repeat your
motions
until i bleed.

not from my veins
but everyplace.

every pore,
every sore,
everything.

remind me of
infinity

by sharing your
life
with me.

**body language.**

let my body say
what my mouth cannot
as i stitch the threads
and untie your knots

let me sink into the
bliss of you
let me kiss every
inch of you

when you and i meet again
words will fade to oblivion
as we misplace where you end
and i begin

**waiting games.**

a flower for each
neuron launched of you,
a paradise born

marcapomaco-
cha, is where i am alone,
imagining you

blue sky and bright life
is what i really think they
aught to be titled

i never want to
live in a cave it isn't
fun at all. at all.

picturing you there
in that kingsized room alone
without your tiger

finding you in the
abyss, our souls form vortices
and there we pass time

**readying.**

the fearless fox
makes ready
by setting up her den

tiger thoughts
are heady
and it's not if but when

she softens the space
sweetens her taste

wriggling into
her kingly lair she
snuggles in and waits

not long now until
again they meet
and time and space abate

in the stars
they play all night
but nothing sweet as this

freedom together
in soft daylight
dissolving into bliss

**behind closed doors.**

these boundary lines of mine
used to be so fluid
even this morning

but inside a lioness
rumbled, protecting me
from myself

protecting you and
what we are

she is fierce
loving
private

and she speaks
loudly
for me to change my tune

and sing softer
quieter
perhaps just for you

and so my vulnerability
goes underground
a bit

because it's none
of their business
and all i want
to do
is love you

without looking
over my shoulder
at what
i might have said

**wanting.**

i run my teeth
gently down the side
of your neck
biting just
a little

kisses along your
collarbone
and the whisper
of my lips
against your
ear

i catch
the crinkle
of your smile

it's been so long

so

long

my mind
is rife
with you
your fingers
and strength

and your
speedy dissolution
into dreams

only to wake again
and ravage me

the wall
awaits
my back

Dear Tiger,

I wonder what makes us this way. Different from others... Not needing a plan or making choices dependent on a future which everyone else seems so attached to but is a fabrication.

What caused the tear in the fabric that few of us can see but through which you and I can glimpse each other so easily?

My egomind loves to make me wrong for this. Loves to try and bring me back to the plane everyone else inhabits. But my soul arises... and the now shimmers deliciously, simmering a stew of moments that end to end add up to a life.

Why do so many need more than a moment? How can we ever obtain more than the truth?

I imagine humidity holding me almost as closely as you. Our sweat mingling. Bodies erased. Obliterated into beautiful oblivion.

The desire which came so quickly has not ever left... but has been building in me slowly like an unseen fire in the mycorrhizal. Underground, unkempt, and unabashed.

In this moment, and for the next and next...

Te quiero, mi tigre.

Travel well, drink deep from the well of life, and come play with me in our dreams.

Tu Zorrita Pequeña

**fantastically real.**

welts linger like stains,
my skin's puckering remains.

i do this to test real,
to ensure that i really feel,
that what this is is true
and that i really do have you.

a sparkling flirtatious start
embedded with poetic art
caused a ripple in me,
something that broke free.

a recentering in my core,
the opening of a once locked door.

your sexy foxy playfulness
makes this parched tiger press
doubting claws deeper into me,
ensuring that this world i see

is our love's true reality
and not just hopeful fantasy.

**drink deep.**

the hours while away
as i fly on cloud cities
away from home

a ditch or hammock
for two would suffice

but for now alone
again with only thoughts
to bring you to me

our souls collide
on this plane and that

i pinch myself blue black
hardly believing my luck

gulping mouthfuls
of this honeyed bliss

thirsty for a time when
our goodbyes end

**thankful.**

you conduct life
with honest integrity,
unapologetic truth,
and unbridled affection.

for this,
i thank you.

you cultivate love
with graceful compassion,
shimmering beauty,
and limitless appreciation.

for this,
i love you.

**blindness.**

wanting to taste you
but there is no haste
or hurry

the flurry of emotions
has turned into
a solid foundation

upon which we build our dreams
and until then
we have our words

which cut like swords
through the rest of life
and leave us breathless

sinking into our
far away sheets
in humid anticipation

in the dark we blindly
fumble for each other
and merge across the ocean

**answers.**

why are my soles so distant
from the ground they yearn to tread

there is nothing more insistent
than your heartbeat in my head

i know we are the space between
the silence, clouds; everything

yet something is set adrift
my heart stays as the plane lifts

stretching strings grow taught
calving my little life apart

glacier melting, soul alight
i see you behind my eyes tonight

our distance is irrelevant
the map of us has treasures yet

the map of us has treasures yet

**lick.**

tracing your skin,
i curiously wander,
as tantalizing sins begin.

excitable exploration of
your fleshy delectability
enkindles our love.

soft, hard, thin, thick,
i paint my lust in
trails slow and quick.

i sneak nibbles and bites,
watching your substance
arc with shuttered delights.

your redolence and taste
pleases my senses,
engorging me with haste.

diving into your flower,
i end my journey and
amp our power.

**ghost.**

my bed is emptier than the sound
echoing inside rounded green bottle edges
rolling on concrete pre-dawn ground

drowsy with champagne dreams of you
laughter bubbles through my lips
my imagination triggers memories
and the arching of my hips

reaching toward your phantom shape
lounging, leaning on sharp elbows
the ghost of you evaporates

left with nothing but to-dos and endless tasks
putting on mask after dutiful mask
i dream of days outside of now
when the sunlit canopy filters across my brow

**playmate.**

pleasurable and delightful
lover of everything.

answering my dreams,
yin to yang.

manifesting beautiful realities,
augmented with fantasies.

teasing all senses,
enkindling my desires.

**thank you.**

how can i express my gratitude
would scrawling words
in trails across the hemispheric sky
be enough

maybe i can crawl into
a cave and emblazon the walls
for anthropologists to interpret
30,000 years from now

or i could learn to teleport
just for you (even if it cost me a decade)
so i could walk across the world
and show up and say it

for now i send pearls that i can't bury
along the heart threads connecting us
heavy raindrops in a dry spell
dusting your shoulders

*Dear Tiger,*

*If you hunger for more, I will happily whet your appetite.*

*Longing for you, my fingers attempt to mimic your technique...
your tongue. But nowhere are your eyes looking up at me
between gulps while you visually relish and physically feast on
my pleasure.*

*I troll my memory banks searching for triggers to help the waves
crest, and there I find you, a threaded hum just below the surface.*

*Tone for tone I want to match you, to merge, to resonate until we
both disappear.*

*So many fantasies to realize. Unlimited potential. A million ways
we haven't yet thought of to quench this saharan thirst.*

*I look forward to systematically checking them each off, marking
them with my tongue one by one along your delicious landscape.*

*Never has my body sung so electric. Never has someone made my
every cell scream. It took you, my forbidden one... to render me
helpless, shaking, obliterated at every seam... It took you.*

*I wasn't supposed to love you. But how could I not fall into the
abyss of pleasure you catapulted me into? How could I not fall
into your heart when you plumbed the depths of mine?*

*Not long ago, you wrote that in you I opened a once locked door.*

*You, my tiger, have blown mine off the hinges.*

**darkness gropes.**

filaments of memory
sketch your contour,
their weightlessness
resurrects your form.

eyes sealed tightly
keeping you real,
only the moonlight tries
washing you away.

in darkness we grope
curves and sticky skin,
heavy breaths mingle
with sweet breezes.

shifting positions distorts
your beautiful hologram,
reassembling you anew
conjures new passions.

mind-shutters oscillate
lascivious memories,
ravaging lust brightens
our inky escapades.

folding and flowing
we detach from reality,
our love explodes celestially
raining bliss eternally.

**aloft.**

heart clogged with
threaded dreams
so many stitches
i couldn't breathe

vacuum sealed
at the seams
my airtight life
begged for teeth

you bit with
meanings of lives
i wrote of cells & slats

which dimmed
our hearty appetites
for anything but [that]

how swiftly
you unraveled me
the rush of blood
felt like wings

in deserted
moonlit majesty
we ripped
the final strings

set adrift
forever free
as playmates
in infinity

**distance dreaming.**

i crawl into my suspended cocoon.
jungle-deep sounds float me away as
crisp summer air refreshes and cools.

though days apart from my love
i am not bereaved but emboldened,
for her love reaches and enraptures me
through lusty and sensual distance dreaming.

**honey.**

there is a moment
when we kiss

the volume changes
desire wells from within

i feel you
drop into me
slowly like a chain
dipped in honey
link by link
sinking seeping
until i'm soaked

there is a moment
when i leave

the toffee strings
of my heart stretch

i feel them
almost snap
they span the
brittle hemispheres
bridging us in
sweetness that
would melt
with the tip
of your tongue

there is a moment
when you return

i imagine and
dissolve into music

i feel days
like decades
march ceaselessly
before me

until again
we are together
and time can
do what it
will without
notice or care

**gifts.**

My life has become a gift wrapped in gratitude.

Everywhere, I see beauty;
in a conversation, a glance,
an energetic pulse exchanged
across the room.

You have given me new eyes
I did not think I needed.

Words spark in the air, bright spots
in private murmurings;
I see your mouth forming them.

My dream of you was a filament
left unlit
until the art of your flesh
and blood and bone
blurred into view

Suddenly
my fragmented path
was crystal clear.

You have gifted me with poetry,
appreciation.

You have shown me my potential,
my supernova self.

From behind the blindfold
I feel your tongue
electric and sing myself
to sleep...

Notes of you hanging in the air
long after the day is done.

**touch.**

Momentary contact,
a brush of human touch
only serves to heighten
my need
for you.

Days pass by
in my cultural
isolation,
handshakes my limited
nourishment.

Nerves thirstily lap
any current or energy
transmission
like the street hounds
who beg for bone & love.

I'm thankful for a few
children and their
curious, innocent touch;
healing and recharging
my depleted reserves.

A usual source of
solace in animals
is lacking due to
flea infestation
or human distrust.

So, I work and wander,
thankful for those
brief fillers and
fleeting encounters
to ease my longing.

I want to be able to
reach for your hand,
your nape, your leg
and pull you close,
escalating with a kiss.

But, for now,
I must content myself
with mental snapshots
and fantasy films
colored with lust.

**a list.**

I sat in (another) airport, waiting to board
watching streams of people flow past me
headed to destinations near and far.

I wonder if they caught
the smile that teased my lips
as I came up with a (partial) list
of things I love about you.

Your...
smile
heart
passion and compassion
temper
dedication
genius
touch
appetite for life
creativity
humor
love of cats (meow).

Your strength
integrity
character
giant physique...

Your capacity to love.

Your voice
beautiful energy
visionary nature.

Your frustration with
our politics and systems.

Your eyes
soft skin and curling hair.

Your l-o-n-g
legs.

Your physical affection
for me.

How we never run out
of things to talk about.

How our bodies fit
like jigsaw pieces.

The names you call me.

Your aesthetic.

The way you look at me.

Your acceptance of
my imperfect life.

Your kindness
generosity
curiosity.

How you taste.

Your sweet tooth.

Your singing =)

How your movements are like song lyrics.
Your poetry.

It's not hard at all
to see why I love you
this much.
The smile teases my lips, still.

**beginnings.**

sitting in stifled light,
surrounded by wandering eyes,
we forget it all
as hands mingle.

too hungry for you
food goes cold,
our only sustenance
each other and wine.

flowing talk gives way
to closer touch,
realizing our direction,
a private location beckons.

i drive, you smile,
you clarify, i jump to the chase,
we scan moonlit cliffs,
searching for suitable shadows.

armrests and console boxes
quickly necessitate a seat shift,
in the unfettered backseat
we voraciously entwine.

falling into a time warp,
we love with friction,
me raw, exhuberant,
you soaked, passionate.

morning dews gather,
realities of life murmur,
final kisses and embrace,
we depart; you north, me east.

temporary is our separation,
as we find time and space
to kindle our passions
and blend our love into one.

**early riser.**

in the morning half-light
my veins pulse with poetry

scarlet words bleed on the page
drop by drop the edges fray

my heavy lidded trance
fills the white spaces

and all i want
is you

**i want to.**

bury you under my weight.
press skin tightly against mine.
mash mouths with lash tongues.
pin wrists, feeling you writhe.
thread fingers, pull hairs.
slide and glide wet flesh.
fold, bend and tightly grip.
lift and enjoy you vertically.
enjoy our mirrored reflections.
taste your charge.
beckon pleasure with motions.
hear ecstasy fill the air.
feel the sun heat us further.
explode inside you.
put us on repeat.

**my turn.**

i want
to drape you in darkness
so my tongue surprises you

to beckon your nerves awake
one by one as i drop
myself unseen into your mouth

to feel your hands range over me
like rivulets over stones

to weave my fingers
through your hair
and pull, burying your moans
with my lips
your rough and unchecked desire
to overtake us both

you to crush me against
the wall, the floor, the bed

you to throw me down
and take nothing but yes

you to make me breathe
fast and ragged

the distance between us
nullified by sweat and skin

**first & last.**

if there is no future and no past
then every day is our first and last
let me linger on your lips
and forever know the taste of this

you slipped into my heart
enwrapped me in a cloak of stars
your needle pulls me close to home
i'm higher than i've ever flown

grateful for the dreamtime travels
where reality unwinds unravels
and you and i can dance again
and infinitely merge lick blend

we swim in air as thick as thieves
solid as the trees and leaves
we breathe like fish with spectral scales
at night we board the astral sails

we take off for lands and seas unknown
fearless because we're not alone
and even when my sleep is broken
i feel you here, my heart wide open

in every waking walking dream
i feel your stitches close my seams
and happy, i come back to life
to each last first time we unite

**demasiado divertido.**

Como boletas de pelo, doblamos riendo,
Cada cosa, cada mira, cada sonido
Estallamos de risa.

Contorsiones llenar el aire
Cuando estamos juntos
Y llenado del amor.

Mis voces, tus frases,
Un perro con torpeza,
O contando una Quechuachitamamacita.

Minuto por minuto,
En cualquier situación
Nos reímos en carcajadas de amor.

Encontramos esta vida
Con aperturas abiertas y suaves
Y seguimos nuestro camino fácil.

Continuamos esta ruta, esta vía,
Y a todos de las chistosas,
Tendremos cada día, cada segundo.

**riovida.**

we go from togetherness
and so many
shared conversations
to nothing so easily
flowing into this
life from that one
and back again
like tides at a
river mouth

the mud from the bottom
stirred
reveals gold
under the turbulence

i wait for you
to flow my way again
you're just around the bend

i press rewind
on the reel of memories
and revel in
the joy of us
knowing that real life
will just put it on
repeat repeat
because we know of
little else
to do but
play

**surgery.**

watching passion cut you
like a knife
i wish i could
suture the wounds

but the only stitches
i can offer are the ones
in our sides
when we laugh
until we ache
with a different
kind of pain

**beneath.**

i lie supine
as sterling stars
sparkle and dash

their density
and immensity
echo our history

rare it is
to enjoy such
dazzling sights

our mindless
programmed progress
erases these moments

may we find
our own paths
outside the race

may we fall
further in love
amidst scenes like these

**secrets.**

you trigger memories
so delicious
i could live on them
for days

my body heats again
as my heart beats again

and i slip into
a dreamy half smile
where everyone who
looks at me
a second time
knows what i'm
thinking

and perhaps wishes
they could be skin
on my skin

like you were
and will be
so soon

no matter...
their eyes
are not what
i want
running down
my back

**t-minus-take-me-down.**

colluding atomic and astral swirls warp
and send us back into each other's reality.
filaments of copper, miles of wireless waves
link us in an eyeblink.

but i want your instantaneousness,
your right-there-in-touch-of-me nowness.
this latest hiccup of distance, our shortest yet,
has thankfully blasted by.

in t-minus-pronto we get to smile, smell, suck and ...
with that i leave us to dream over the night's darkness
and ever impending dawn.

sin ti, mi mundo parace menos delicioso.
contigo, nuestro mundo es riquisimo.

**thankfully so.**

thank you,
sun,
earth,
moon,
air/water/ice.

you, too,
life,
love,
giggles,
and all things nice.

my family,
mom,
dad,
sis,
and all the rest.

my fox,
light,
love,
playmate,
and all things best.

my friends,
pals,
amigos,
open hearts,
fellow mischiefers.

my teachers,
guides,
lovers,
strangers,
and wise ancestors.

thank you,
to the soul
powering my
material shell.

offerings to gaia
for the food that
nourishes and
keeps me well.

a tip-of-the-hat
to comedy,
error, and
the ever unknown.

a playful tickle
to our fears,
preoccupations, and
seeds yet sown.

thank you to
those discovering
truth, beauty,
grace.

and an appreciation
for technology,
inventions and
the silly rat race.

a cheers to all
religions,
mighty and small.

hearty blessings and glee
to those not
exactly like me.

thank you anonymity
and her cousin,
community.

a high five to stimulation,
adrenaline,
surprise and titillation.

mil gracias a los peruanos,
¡mis bacanes paisanos
adoptivos!

a love for art,
expression, and
everything from the heart.

a hug to life,
a kiss to death.
appreciation for endings,
and new breaths.

to the creepies,
and cuties.
the softies,
and crawlies.

from the teeny
to infinity.

but most of all
from me
to thee.

**¡vámonos!**

I see through the handsome mask
your soul wears by day.

Your dreams and poetry penetrate
my smallness
and make me believe bigger things
of myself,
of the world.

My sleeping desires are awake...
My heart illuminates the path ahead.

I tread without fear
knowing my feet will land
in the right place.

Walls they'd build to lovingly cage us
have footholds
we could find blindfolded.

Besides, the truth
shining through our skin
is always free.

We'll launch ourselves over
without backward glance,
leaving pieces of our hearts
to those who can't understand.

**welcome home.**

she stood blindfolded
waiting for him

strangers walked past
whispering
not so quietly

her pulse
r
a
c
e
d

shaky hands
held his
bold instructions

his bags
dropped
beneath black silk
she spied his shoes
step toward her

into his arms
he swept her
as she smiled
into his lips

and they all
applauded
the audacity
of public
declarations

**i promise.**

to speak the truth
and laugh hysterically
from the floor or
not
enjoying every drop
of you

to always seek love
in darkness
and find it
in each other

to only run
up mountains
and never away
from reality
(unless we ride
together
on a unicorn)

to voice
my desires
and understand
we might not
always inhabit
the same
wavelength

to share all of me
with all of you

to listen
learn
wonder
appreciate
skip
fuck
reach

ask
touch

to take
care of myself
and you and us

to be trustworthy
and lustworthy
(less bacon
may be in order)

to cultivate curiosity
and revel in what is

to stay until we make
another choice
or don't

in this moment and that
and that
to love you

**sweetness.**

who, how, or why
was sweetness
crafted?

what molecular
dance unfolded
to make it so?

or was it a
godly
prophesy?

a demand for
an energy
enricher?

was matter
and light
craving more?

scientists
might simply say,
*"evolution."*

i want to
dream a richer
possibility.

sweetness is
an updraft of
brilliance.

a soft and
caressing love
of life
shattering
banality with
gentle throbs.

to be sweet
is to give
everything.

sweetness is
the power of life
bitesized.

it can even
deflate
death.

its power
lingers in
fragrance.

hypnotizing
distractions
its norm.

delight and
mirth are its
companions.

if its origins
are ho-hum or
otherworldly,

all i will
attest to
is that
sweetness is
everything you
are to me.

**annual.**

i've enjoyed the
twisting, turning
morph of unknown
stranger into
fully known
lover.

a year ago
we exchanged
digital notes
that crescendoed
into eight hours
of foggy car windows.

my, how some years pass.

our early exchanges,
transitioning into
bi-weekly trysts,
filled my heart
with brilliant
shine.

extending my
stay was perfect,
not just for the sex,
but for soldering bonds
with laughs, thermal baths
and star-sprinkled desert nights.

*why is it always so fun?*

not one,
but two long
distance trips to
see me spoke volumes
of who you are and what
i mean to you.

full of ease,
white light, beauty,
and hilarity, you
remind me of a slim
Gummi Bear full of
Gummi Juice.

come bounce with me.

thank you for a
wonderful year.

a year of incredible
distance, yet filled,
already, with incredible
memory.

may we share,
and explore,
and dance,
and discover,
and devour
many more.

**roots.**

you pulled me
across the world
rendering me
snowblind
with eyes
only for our new
life

(the one i couldn't see before)

i didn't think that list
i made at eighteen
could ever
be embodied

yet
here you are

the dreams
i always had
stretch their legs
and run

to me you
are sunlight
oxygen
dark loamy
soul food
for fresh roots
plunging madly

thank you for
polishing my shine
for stabbing me
with aching laughter
for making this
so easy

for being yourself
always
which is the only
thing i want

**slow.**

the words once came
fast and furious

they've slowed
now that every day
reads
like a poem

yet the rarity of us
is rendered in
every outside glance

making forgetfulness
impossible

I savor the
universe of you...
who
rearchitected
my heart
into a shelter
full of oxygen

day after day
I steep in
leaves of gratitude

every morning
we reinvent
our fusion

alchemists
of truth and beauty

eternal reminders
that
this is
possible

**settling for unsettling.**

thankfully, our past lives
have already haunted us.

we chased perfection,
settled for safe 'n easy.

we tried molding ourselves
to perceived expectations.

we sidelined our inner
artists in favor of normal.

now, with words still un
spoken, we tread on.

unknown.
in love.

no longer restrained by
acceptable limitations
we build a nest
embodied pure love.

we craft a lifestyle
that invites inclusion.

we enjoy laughing,
discovering, & loving.

whatever it is.
i say yes.

**namaste.**

we are gods
in material shells
deciding daily
to live in heaven or hell

my skin changes
but i stay the same
i try not to suffer
when i writhe with pain

for the wolves and the
monkeys, lions, and bears
our wildness uncovered
layer by layer

stay true to the light
and the miracular

aim true in the night
stars spectacular

i'll be with you though
thankfully so

even when my eyes forget
and my heart becomes lead

forever and always
the divine in me
will truly see

# exquisite corpse.

*22 lines // alternating writers line by line // sight unseen*

junkfish dances alone
the trees in winter
shimmery silvery seduction
sprawling like green tomatoes
cuttle-n cuddle tight
i miss you when you're like this

rupturing venomous thought
shootingstar spectaular
esctatic renderings blossom
and then i wake up

while rudimentary cripples party
my blue gray mornings
forgetting wild transgressions
dipped in rose water

fritting while transporting taste
scented like love potion no. 9
holding through shape shift
divine like straight sugarcane

dropped withering tangibles
i drink you in
without secretive contract
and toast to our supernova

**outside my window.**

i see you in him
the raven
that hesitates
at the edge of the roof
looking down
and forgetting
that he already knows
how to fly

and suddenly he
leaps
easier than breathing
steadier on his wings
than he
ever was on his feet

**an inkling of a smidgeon.**

moochie woochie woo!
that's how much i love you.

some may be unable to tell
but you, my dear, see our spell.

we galavant like whimsical creatures
never hiding our animal features.

some may dismiss or wish us away
but by your side i long to stay.

our ebbs always turn into flows
that's how fluid our vacation goes.

thank you for unleashing the real you
for you uncaged a beast with love so true.

**currents.**

you were made for me
stardust i recognize
a poem in form
swimming toward me
like a monsoon
i'd dive into you
any day
because
i've grown gills
and you
give me oxygen

**infinite webbing.**

the belly of our
passion
wants
soft-eyed vigilance

hazy focus
lazy love

truth
runs deeper
than feelings
an underground river
rushing
everpresent

skate the surface
like gelatin
never sinking

watch
with
heavy lidded
eyes

as we drape on
brief costumes
of griefenvy
angerbliss
joyregret

a pretty
catastrophic
picture show

clickclacking
whirspinning
brightly lit
distractions

desperately
seeking forgetfulness
of

one

single

truth:

we are bright spots
on an infinite thread

webbing the universe
together like starpoints

**tantra.**

revelation
asks
for nothing

so lay awhile
with the power
of your softness

remember
to
breathe

steep in the
soothing strength
of allowing
everything

slide your lips
slowly
along saltlines

slick skin
silkens
under rapt
attention

beauty seeps
into openings
if you let it

**lightlove.**

soul awakening
rushes in
slamming
like a weightless
ton of bricks

blowing through you
like glitter

torn
a  p  a  r  t
made
whole electric

you are a
black hole
ecstatic
abyss

**infinite shine.**

ego divides us
a corridor separates us
continents have distanced us
time disperses us

but love links us
a twin flame flickers
no matter the fathoms
no matter the dark

no matter
you and i are
infinite shine

**containing.**

I am not
just a vessel
for your love.

I hold your pain,
your shame.

Your darkness
can come and live
with me for awhile
so you
can
rest.

Because I have room
for all of you.

By now our eyes
have seen so much
of each other,
but I never tire
of the view.

Because I have room
for all of you.

You remind me
of how beautiful
flaws can be.

You remind me of the gold
in my own cracks.

You fill my own spaces
so well,

because I have room
for all of you.

**never two much.**

two years,
fast and molasses,
today and back
to today.

we've kept
pace
through a
torrent of love.

many secretly
thought,
"nah, it won't
last."

some wanted
us to slow
down, that we
were too much.

but we thanked,
and then forgot
their fears
as we looked at ours.

on the start
of our next
infinite
journey.

i want to
remind you
over and over
that it's you

i love.

## the dreamchanger.

you changed your dreams
for me

in a whirlwind
of love you
pulled me
and my child
close
claiming us

you plied
open
my fearful heart
as we left
an unwritten future

and scrawled a
new one
together

our house
floods with
my heart

you
and your hands
command
me
to open
still

and i will
open for you
for the rest of my days

**stargazer.**

i feel her
in my belly

starry
sacred
swooshing
sweetness

that we made
together

this girlchild
this love
this life
this everything
seems surreal sometimes

i didn't know
before we met
that i dreamed
too small

**taste.**

flavorfull, llena con amor.
sensual delectibility
trickles down my throat.

catching you in the
crevices
for a second, third taste.

encapsulate, preserve.
nothing can capture
the flesh bliss of you.

**beautiful night.**

a glorious still
seventy-two degrees.

scent of
practice lingers.
foreign,
now home.

steps and
routine.

much easier
with a cousin.

much lovelier
with a twin flame.

**An Intro to El Cuentito.**

To keep our long-distance love alive, we played many creative games during the ten months we lived apart (including publishing all of these poems anonymously on a poetry blog, surprising each other with new poems every so often).

The story on the following pages, "El Cuentito," was written exquisite corpse style... Tigre began the story with four sentences, but only let Lola see the last two lines, from which she had to continue the tale.

She shared only the last two sentences of her portion back to him, and so the story was written... bit by bit, over the span of a few months.

Though we only could "see" half the story, when all the lines were revealed at the end, what unfolded was a fantastical short story of a man on a mystical quest. It sounds and reads as though it was written by one being.

We hope you enjoy this tale of love, timelessness, and shamanic magic.

# el cuentito

*an exquisite corpse short story*

The sweaty ceiling drips incessantly with a, "plink, plink, plink," as I lie awake in my hammock. Breathing the dense evening air feels like sucking on a smoothie with a straw too small. All I can think about is how similar tonight is to the one I try to keep alive. I'd like to think that my latest patchwork version is accurate, but one can never know given the fallibility of the human mind...

... as I wrestle myself away from dreamy half-sleep and transition into the greygroggy pre-dawn morning, I wonder if I'll ever know which of my lives is real. I wipe the crusty yellow remnants of midnight from my eyes and push off the crackling covers. Small blue sparks of static sweep across the duvet - last vestiges of the energy which undoubtedly erupted from my skin as I wracked through another torturously sleepless night, wondering fruitlessly why my life has been cobbled together into countless and unending iterations.

Explosions echo in the distance, shredding my attempts at recollection. I fling off the thin and ragged duvet and release myself from my self confinement. I don my only clothing: a yellow t-shirt, rust stained jeans and my old, but trusty, campesino shoes given to me by a Colombian friend. Leaving the room, I slip into the hallway down the dark, musty corridor. Moonlight sprinkles in through slats in the walls with her soft glow, easing my fractured thoughts.

I can't tell if it's day or night anymore; which life I'm living. The schizophrenic split between the realities I inhabit is getting more pronounced each day. Shaking my head and no longer trusting any of my senses, I make my way toward an early breakfast when a sudden, sharp pain seizes my right ankle and my knees buckle under the enormous weight of electric terror. A shiny beaded spider drops from the leg of my jeans and shimmies along the floor, looking back with triumph as I sink to my knees with an empty stomach and a hollow sense of dread.

Years of living in the backcountry and many visits to exotic places like the Amazon have exposed me to a variety of death-inducing creatures. Black widows, rattlers, brown recluses and scorpions have occupied our land since long before we called it home (I've been stung by the latter, twice; a pain that pales compared to this), so I'm used to being around imminent suffering or potential death.

*But this is something else.* I am still glued to the ground in pain... venomous and searing heat courses up my leg into my pelvis and expands in all directions.

A sound must have escaped me as I crumpled and my lover Esperanza turns the corner and rushes to my side, her face mirroring the pain that must be apparent on mine.

"We've got to get you to a hospital, amor."

"I don't think we have time," I gasp as I double over on my side... the blood rushing behind my eyes renders everything red and filmy in the husky light. Esperanza's face goes blank, bile rises into my throat, and the familiar feeling of erasure takes hold as my head hits the earthen floor.

For a short while, unconsciousness claims my mind. Minutes, or hours, I cannot say with certainty, pass and the hazy emptiness slowly transitions to a dream world that feels familiar and real.

I'm standing, alone and devoid of any recognizable trait. My characteristic black, wavy hair is replaced with nothingness; my all-too visible scars decorating my left side have vanished into smooth ambiguity — I am myself, but also an anonymous something watching a new world being born around me.

The sights and sounds permeate my nothingness and the overwhelming sensations would be beyond comprehension if I had a mind to process it all. But I am now a part of it, emerging and fading as my molecules spread apart and dissipate into it all.

The sense of peace that arises upon the evaporation of my mindbody can't be expressed in words.

As the me that is no longer self observes and joins my surroundings, I possess all knowledge and no thoughts. Then, into the stillness of a new earth, I am born again.

Tranquility distills my essence and sensations of love-drenched light illuminate—with exacting clarity—a universe of infinite possibility. The thoughts of pain, terror and wretched dissolution of my terrestrial body are no longer a foe or interminable threat.

I watch, not with eyes transmitting light into electro-impulses, but with all of my being. Examining the spectacular alien fauna and flora filling every vista, they watch and communicate with me without sound, only thought.

It's like this every time I dissolve, and it's almost always triggered by trauma.

When my first wife left me, I quite literally erased myself; disappearing from our world for what turned out to be the perfect length of time to get over the heartbreak.

Of course the "I" that was heartbroken was no more (in time or form at least), and when I re-entered the earth plane again, centuries had passed and my fairly new soul was confused by innovations my eyes and brain could not have possibly processed.

When I resurface this time, I know I will wonder what happened to my packed earth homestead and my beautiful amiguita from this most recent life that I'd come to love.

In a flash of seconds, the tantalizing dance of flora and fauna gives way to dissonant chaos as life before my reforming eyes becomes disappointingly familiar.

The noise and newness of this place feels like torture. Distractions, luring flashes of light, horrible horns and impatient faces surround me. I hope that this isn't where I am destined to land. Fighting through this madness to shape a home is tantamount to torture.

I am shaken when I start feeling the familiar sensations of human experience creep back in, and feel the distance growing between myself and the omnipresence I felt before. Hunger is the first earthly sensation I am burdened with, followed by thirst.

As people pass in mindless monotones, I push my hands into pockets I find by my side and locate some foreign coins and bills crumpled in them.

I often wonder whether anyone notices my sudden appearances... or perhaps they don't see me at all; my materialization being far outside of their brains' grid cell processing capabilities.

It is strange to be inserted first into form, and second into function.

Each time I appear, I am the same wavy-haired, scarred man, with centuries of love and heartbreak built like bricks inside my mortared, wounded soul. A familiar feeling of dizzying loss, hunger, thirst, and lust infuses my synapses, shooting lighting electricity through my body, propelling me to quickly seek something to eat, someone to love, and anything to quench the restlessness that accompanies my constant search for home.

Heaviness and dread walk with me as I search for sustenance. What seems to be a restaurant on my left is decently packed with clientele, a marquee above the door has 'Disfrute' written in a script font. It's the closest I can translate into a Romance language, but would read in English as 'Enjoy.'

Walking into the eatery I take note of the queue of people in front of what appears to be a large menu in the same elegant, yet approachable, handwriting as the sign outside. I join the line and try to discern what my eating options are based on my paltry change and ravenous hunger. I strain to overhear each person's order to judge what might be the local fare to avoid any inappropriate choices.

My options are pretty limited, but everyone seems to be ordering a side of the homestyle bread, so I order three rolls and make my way to a low wooden table. As I sit down and tear into the slightly sour and delicious bread, I start trying to put together the pieces of when and where I am. People are speaking together in quiet, hushed tones. The restaurant feels warm and homey, bathed in the soothing sounds of lovers' conversations. It brings to memory hundreds of evenings I've had before, making this time and place difficult to identify.

I catch myself following their words of adoration, fidelity and future plans. One woman is describing their first kiss beneath her family's fig tree in the backyard; another lover lavishes praise for his partner's wonderful parenting of their three precious children.

I know that I've lived these lives, or at least I feel deep down that their lives were mine. The confusion of these dozen or so moments starts to overwhelm my senses, and my eyes begin to slowly close when "CLANK!" – a plate of food resembling potatoes, lentils and a creamy sauce hits my table and shatters the heavy mental blanket shutting me down.

I wonder where this plate of food came from, since I only had enough money for bread and butter. I search the restaurant to see who my anonymous benefactor might be. To my left, a hearty-looking gentleman digs into his own similar plate and nods in my direction with a smile.

Since I'm never one to let generosity go unacknowledged, I take a break from devouring the steaming food to get up and thank him for buying the rest of my dinner. People seem to be speaking some sort of Spanish dialect here, so I start to speak in my own halting Spanish. He puts his hand up to stop me, breaks into a friendly smile and says in English, "You're welcome" in a warm baritone, gesturing for me to sit down... I get a distinct sense that somehow this man knows me.

His hands have the look of many lives lived, much like the lives inside my head. The blunt fingertips almost swallow the stubby fingernails as they rap a slow, syncopated beat with the ceiling fan's "whir-whir-whir" above us.

"Why did you come here?" he asks me, again in English with only a hint of a foreign accent.

"Why did I come here?" I repeat inside my head. What an odd question to ask, *as if I've ever been able to control my scattered celestial leaps.* He continues his fingertip tap dance, looking me straight in the eye with the corners of his mouth curling up as if he already knows my response.

The simplest answer is that I was famished when I re-materialized, hence my choice to immediately satiate my hunger with the few crumpled bills in my pockets. The more complicated answer? Why my cells chose this time and place in which to reappear? That is an answer that I myself am seeking...

"I actually don't know how much choice I had in the matter," I explained as the man nodded in warm collusive understanding - as if we were part of some cosmic criminal conspiracy.

Given his response, I dare to continue on with more detail.

"I never quite know what precipitates my departure nor how my cells decide where I will manifest... the only thing I know for sure is that every time I leave, I leave my life behind completely, and I'm not sure if the earth I come back to is the same one from which I left... there is not much I'm sure of anymore."

The man relaxes in his chair, taking a sip of his drink without breaking eye contact. He continues his stare. Without the dissonance of the surrounding chatter, it would be tempting to think that time has stopped.

But, before I can end this awkward silence and thank him for his generosity, he says, "I know how to stop it, but where you finally land I have no say."

"You know how to stop this constant flipping of worlds and existences?" I quickly reply.

I've always dreamed of halting the convulsions of time and place, but never believed it possible, nor did I have a clue that there might be others sharing my fate.
"Yes, but like I said, I can't determine where, who or how you'll end up," the increasingly enigmatic man replied.

My heart pounds slowly and solidly in my chest as I think about the possibility of a settled life. A life where I don't have to fear putting down roots that won't be painfully ripped from under me the minute a traumatic event triggers another cellular dissolution.

The idea resonates, but, as with anything unknown, brings with it a certain amount of fear. Irrational thoughts flit through at lightning speed while I slowly consume my meal... What if I don't fit in where I land? What if I never find love again? What if I still feel out of place and don't have my pre-built escape route anymore? What if I still feel empty... Perhaps I would finally have to learn to sustain myself, work which I'd long been avoiding; conveniently distracted by the continual explosion and reconstruction of my atoms over these many years.

My spoon hovers over my last bite as my thoughts massage my potential future. This mouthful of nourishment is keeping me from solidifying my decision. I know that with its swallow, I'll be forced to make a decision: stay the course of repeated atomic reconstruction, or follow this man into a permanent unknown.

I scoop the last from my plate and work it over in my mouth. The pieces disintegrate with each chew and automatic toss of my tongue. My meal finished, I put my utensil down, wipe my mouth and look at my companion.

"Let's end this roller coaster. What do I need to do?" I ask.

"We must first go for a walk," the man softly replies.

I get up slowly, my body still full of aches and pains from rematerializing. I wonder whether I'll begin to heal when I arrive at my "final" destination - to live a life without this constant dull ache would feel like sheer bliss.

We step outside of the restaurant and into the purple evening. My companion walks beside me, gripping my elbow as we navigate the dusty, rutted street.

"Where should we go?" I somewhat nervously inquire.

"There is a vortex point just beyond town on that ridge over there. It may take us awhile to get there, but that's where we need to be."

"Should we catch a taxi for part of the way? The shape we're in, it's going to take hours to get there."

"No, we need to wear out our bodies to the point of exhaustion. The only way for this to work is to completely give in... to surrender in total. And so, we'll walk. We should be there at the perfect time. There's a lunar eclipse tonight at 2:22am. I'm aiming to be there by then. Let's go."

Walking in new-old bodies is always an awkward experience at first. The kinetics of my previous form carries over in what I assume is the nebulous anti-matter of my memory. That same memory that allows me to recall my various prior states of existence.

Fortunately, or unfortunately, those same memories have faded with passing years (or has it been eons I've experienced life in this manner?). Recall of past existence is usually prompted by smells, tastes and other physical sensations, like now, walking in *this* body, with my stranger companion, towards this vortex-portal-thing so very far away.

Twilight begins to fall as we make our way out of town and start navigating the rough, scrubby terrain at the long, scree-filled flank of the ridge. Normally temperatures don't phase me much, but whether it's the pending dusky drop in temperature or the delicious unknown ahead, I tremble slightly and my teeth start to chatter.

We walk for hours in silence, next to each other, each in our own thought worlds. I wonder what my strange companion is thinking as he carefully steps over low, scratchy chaparral.

*How many people has he taken on this journey? How many others before me have struggled with staying put in one body or decade? How many people have left countless lovers and painful traumas only to awake in another, similar but different dream?*

The desiccating milieu leaves me thirsty for a refreshment. At times I lag slightly behind, encumbered by my large frame and a few excessive pounds of flesh. My guide patiently waits for me to catch up as we scramble dusty, crumbling granite turned scree. With each thirsty thought of water, I try to remind myself of a days-long hike with a spiritual maestro some 15 or so life experiences back. We survived without water (or food) for two days, and with our destination creeping closer and closer, I mentally reset my need for water like that teacher taught me.

Somehow, the uncertainty of whether I'll actually emerge alive from this experience seems to further quell my thirst. *If I don't survive, why worry about my paltry thirst here and now?*

The terrain steepens as witching-hour darkness envelopes us with her dry, brisk embrace. As we near the top of the ridge, I feel currents of energy surge through my body.

The moonshadow begins to fade with the impending eclipse and I know 2:22 is near. My companion motions to me to follow him to a clearing surrounded by three boulders, each the size of a small car. He lays his poncho on the ground and motions for me to sit. Apparently, the ritual is beginning. My breathing quickens as the eclipse approaches its apex.

Sitting cross-legged, I shut my eyes and begin to cleanse my mind of thought and ego. I recall my past life traveling with an indigenous shaman in Nepal and his techniques for meditation. Watching the internal dialogues float as if they are passing clouds allows me to see them as the transient and temporary things they really are.

A vibrational intensity begins to flow into the space we're occupying. My body doesn't sense a specific direction the vibrations are coming from; they seem to be engulfing us from an infinity of directions. My eyes are shut, but I feel my third eye opening… taking in the hallucinogenic visions and colors that are beginning to fill the space. Colors of the rainbow start shifting and morphing into new ones I've never seen. Hues with complexity and multidimensional character form song-like structures that begin resonating with the intensified physical vibrations hugging my physical being.

As the vibrations strengthen, I begin to feel an almost orgasmic sensation as my body begins to transform from solid matter into what seems and feels like beams of pure white light. The only visual input comes to me through my 6th chakra, as the solid matter of me completely evaporates.

A wash of utter peace and joy enwrap what's left of "me". *Why did I ever worry that this process would cause my death or would somehow leave me feeling alone at my destination?* The futility of fear is so clear to me now that if I could ring out with joyous laughter, I would.

**I am love, I am everything, I am the universe.**

I can see myself in the stars, feel the heat of me in the sunlight and sense the freshness of me within every molecule of oxygen.

I want to capture this feeling of bliss, but my human desire to *cling* forces the air around me to compress, and I am sucked through time and space; plunging into a cold, metal room with no windows.

*"I told you, the key is surrender...."* A voice echoes in my mind.
*"Surrender absolutely or you'll travel to the underworld before you can walk the earth again."*

The powerful sensation of dissolution is absorbed and stolen from me by the lifelessness of my new surroundings. My bodiless being has returned to what appears to be a material world.

"Oh shit," I think to myself, "Did it not work? Am I in another one of my endless lives? And why am I alone?"

My mind runs through these and other questions, trying to reassemble the bliss I sensed... the feeling of total inclusion and happiness, but, *"Why am I here?"* is all that floats to the surface.

The only remnants of myself before the 'uptake' is my consciousness and my seated position. My skin is now even more heavily scarred, as if I've suffered burns upon burns. The damage, from what I can see, seems to extend all over my body. I turn my hands over to examine my palms and notice small, deep holes. As I bring my hand closer for inspection I begin to notice small, translucent, worm-like animals are inhabiting the vacancies in my skin. Quickly, I turn my hands over to forget their presence, but it fails to work as I begin to feel their small, undulating raspings against my nerves. I feel like screaming from the intense discomfort and terror their multitudes manifest.

My mouth opens and an involuntary spasmodic sound escapes my throat. The creatures are stirring under my skin, moving up my arms and down into my chest cavity. I shudder and shake, trying to escape from the torture taking place inside me. The more I resist them, the faster and more intensely they seem to travel.

I try to calm myself, hoping that if I slow my reactions down, they will become less manic and eventually dissipate. But, I can't catch a deep breath to help bring me focus. Every time I inhale, it feels like the pointed tips of steak knives are twisting into the top of my lungs by way of my clavicle. Thoughts start circulating and a new mantra takes place of the panic. Over and over again, the only thought I have is *Fuck this!* Fuck my "friend" for tempting me with this journey. *Fuck me for my apparent hellish fate. Just kill me already and be done with it...* I'm not sure how much more of this I can take.

Pressures of pain continue filling my every sensation. A stench of chemical toilets permeates my sinuses and lays a caustic blanket over my mucous membranes. The backs of my eyes feel like they're being peeled from the inside as my vision short circuits in brilliant stabs of bright light. The sheer sensation of every nerve being violated and severely molested brings about a state of delirium.

I keep expecting shock to overtake my body and let me pass peacefully to the endless everythingness, but I'm left violently shaking on the cold floor. I salivate uncontrollably and drool on the floor as my head mops itself in it. A sliver of my "normal" self sits in the corner of my mind watching it all take place. I find refuge in this detached part of myself in an attempt to fight off the overwhelming oppression of pain. My mind flashes in electrified shocks, pulling me writhing and shrieking from my escape. I'm placed in the epicenter of all the pain. For the first time since arriving to this place of suffering, I feel a presence and sense that I'm not alone.

The metal room tangs with a sudden absence of pain and noise. The tinning sound subsides like tuning forks and I squint as blinding white light floods the space. My hands involuntarily clutch at my eyes, any pain or inability to move forgotten as I react to the sudden, intrusive blindness.

As the light subsides, it pulsates in tempo with my faintly beating heart... no longer able to sustain a state of fight or flight, my body has finally gone into a state of frozen shock; my pulse is faint, but steady... matching beat for beat with the disappearing brightness. I wonder what place this is; where the inputs now seem to match my biochemical and physiological states. Perhaps, if I can regain control of my systems and release into an infantile state of intuitive trust, I will be able to escape whatever time-warp, wormhole prison I've landed in.

"*Exactly*," a whisper permeates from somewhere inside my head.

Startled, I move my shaking hands away from my eyes and look for the voice's source. No one is nearby, but I do notice that my metallic entrapment has seemingly given way to another space altogether. I am no longer lying in a pool of my own desperate saliva, but by the side of a clear stream.

Soft grasses brush and flow against my fetal form gently washing away the brutal memories of my prior physical torment. I reach to feel my most recent wounds to find them non-existent. My body is intact, I am no longer wracked with nausea-inducing pain. Fearful to put my faith and trust in the current "reality," I continue to lie in the grass, the stream noiselessly slinking past, and breathe. After a few deep cycles and sighs of relief, I start to sit up.

Looking around my surroundings, I'm relieved to not see a single sign of man's creations. There is no concrete, no buildings, nothing metal or extracted. Only nature accompanies me here. The air is warm, I'm guessing the climate is mid to late summer, somewhere temperate judging by the lack of strong humidity and the willow looming over me, drinking from the passing stream. Still overwhelmed by my painful torture, sensing I'm in a safe space, I lie down and enter a deep slumber.

For the first time in weeks, maybe decades, I sleep soundly. My ruptured and broken body has craved rest since before I can remember and my mind and memory have never let me have it. My existence is infused with calm and peace, where once only lived chaos and pain.

Not even a dream would dare puncture this unbroken blissful rest. Time seems to pass, and a slight chill to the breeze finally rouses me. Through the bowed branches, I glance a sliver of moon hanging low over the horizon, just above a band of fading gold. I stretch along the ground, surprised at the ease with which I can bring my arms overhead. I bring my hands down, inspecting them for traces of the creatures who, not long ago, were eating me from the inside out. I see nothing but strong, calloused skin - that of a well-worn farmer. Marveling, my eyes travel upwards along my arms, and the scars that once ravaged my left side and most recently, my entire body, are nowhere in sight.

Stars begin winking from ages past. Mars' red pulse grows brighter and stronger as I continue lying on my back and absorbing the serene diversion the expansiveness offers... Soft, calming winds glide across me and I watch the tall grasses become harder and harder to see against the inky everythingness.

Lying in peace and realizing I'm safe, for now, I start to feel myself fading again into blissful sleep. My body jolts awake once, as if I'm free-falling on a fast roller coaster, and then slumber finally begins to set in.

Dreams start forming behind my shuttered eyelids; flashes of color leaping and dancing to a silent synapse symphony. A red webbed sphere emerges from the borealis and spins slowly in my mind, shrinking and growing as it seems to move through my memories.

The red sphere suddenly glows white, expands infinitely, and from its center, I can make out the shape of a woman emerging. As her form clarifies, she begins to walk toward me; her face shifting like a viewmaster through a tantalizingly familiar slide-show of my lost lovers' faces. She grows more beautiful as she transmutes from Amelia to Zephyr to my countless other part-ners from my former time-shift existence. She settles on the ap-pearance of my last love... my greatest love; Esperanza, who I left behind in a rammed-earth hallway - her memory of me irrevers-ibly erased the minute I disappeared...

Joy, love and happiness flood my body. I stare into those crys-tal azul eyes as they lay their beauty on mine. The entity appear-ing as Esperanza reaches her hands out, beckoning me to walk towards her.

I take steps toward her. As I walk I feel that familiar disso-lution of my body taking place, but this time it's different. My mind is still present, and this warm and loving form isn't shifting and distorting, nor is my mind melting and bending like usual, preparing me for my latest incarnation. Taking my last steps, I raise my arms to meet hers and see that my material essence is transforming to an illuminated ash. I look down at my feet and they're melting like grains of sand pouring from a bucket and are spreading across the floor.

I make eye contact with Esperanza and as I watch the tip of my nose dissolve into the ether, I hear her say, "Suffer no more."

The vision of her also starts to drain like the innards of an hourglass, and we both dissipate downward, our particles merg-ing in a glowing pool directly under where our feet stood just moments before. An incredible feeling of bliss washes through my consciousness, and suddenly I can feel not only Esperanza's true nature, but the nature of every conscious being in the uni-verse.

Our molecules continue to blend and dance, now forming an

infinite, spinning torus. As the beauty and purity of universal consciousness washes through me, I recognize that I'll never suffer again. I'm no longer in a body that will repeatedly experience painful and discordant deaths. I feel certain that I'll no longer have to say goodbye to the ones I love, for in actuality I cannot ever leave them - we are already a part of each other.

I never again have to be tortured over the latest destructive human actions - I can see clearly that the end result will still be this feeling of bliss, no matter what happens in the interim. That this incomprehensible love is the only truth... I have nothing to worry about, nothing to fear; I am nothing and I am everything.

The feeling stays as I open my eyes and feel the grass beneath my back.

I am free.

*fin.*